GAO

Report to the Subcommittee on Military Construction, Veterans Affairs, and Related Agencies, Committee on Appropriations, U.S. Senate

May 2012

DEFENSE INFRASTRUCTURE

Documentation Lacking to Fully Support How DOD Determined Specifications for the Landstuhl Replacement Medical Center

GAO

Accountability ★ Integrity ★ Reliability

GAO
Accountability * Integrity * Reliability

Highlights

Highlights of GAO-12-622, a report to the Subcommittee on Military Construction, Veterans Affairs, and Related Agencies, Committee on Appropriations, U.S. Senate

DEFENSE INFRASTRUCTURE

Documentation Lacking to Fully Support How DOD Determined Specifications for the Landstuhl Replacement Medical Center

Why GAO Did This Study

Landstuhl Regional Medical Center (LRMC) is DOD's only tertiary medical center in Europe that provides specialized care for servicemembers, retirees, and their dependents. Wounded servicemembers requiring critical care are medically evacuated from overseas operations to the 86th Medical Group clinic at Ramstein Air Base to receive stabilization care before being transported to LRMC for intensive care. According to DOD, both facilities were constructed in the 1950s and are undersized to meet current and projected workload requirements. DOD plans to consolidate both facilities into a single medical center at an estimated cost of $1.2 billion. In this report, GAO (1) describes how DOD considered changes in posture and the beneficiary population when developing facility requirements, (2) assesses DOD's process for determining facility requirements, and (3) reviews DOD's process to develop the facility's cost estimate. GAO examined posture planning documentation, beneficiary demographic data, plans for the replacement medical center, and relevant DOD guidance, as well as interviewed relevant DOD officials.

What GAO Recommends

GAO recommends that DOD provide clear and thorough documentation of how it determined the facility's size and cost estimate, correct any calculation errors, and update its cost estimate to reflect these corrections and recent posture changes. In commenting on a draft of this report, DOD concurred with GAO's recommendations and stated that it has conducted a reassessment of the project that will be released once approved by the Secretary of Defense.

View GAO-11-622. For more information, contact James R. McTigue, Jr. at (202) 512-7968 or mctiguej@gao.gov or Debra A. Draper at (202) 512-7114 or draperd@gao.gov.

What GAO Found

Department of Defense (DOD) officials considered current beneficiary population data, contingency operations, and most of the expected changes in troop strength when planning for the replacement medical center. However, recently announced posture changes in January 2012 have yet to be assessed for their impact on the facility. DOD estimates that the replacement medical center will provide health care for nearly 250,000 beneficiaries. A majority of those who are expected to receive health care from the center come from within a 55-mile radius of the facility. DOD officials told us that because the replacement medical center was designed for peacetime operations—with the capacity to expand to meet the needs of contingency operations—reductions in ongoing contingency operations in Afghanistan would not have an impact on facility requirements. At the time of this review, DOD officials said they were in the process of assessing proposed changes in posture to better understand their possible impact on the sizing of the replacement medical center.

DOD officials incorporated patient quality of care standards as well as environmentally friendly design elements in determining facility requirements for the replacement medical center. DOD also determined the size of the facility based on its projected patient workload. Internal control standards require the creation and maintenance of adequate documentation, which should be clear and readily available for examination to inform decision making. However, GAO's review of the documentation DOD provided in support of its facility requirements showed (1) inconsistencies in how DOD applied projected patient workload data and planning criteria to determine the appropriate size for individual medical departments, (2) some areas where the documentation did not clearly demonstrate how planners applied criteria to generate requirements, and (3) calculation errors throughout. Without clear documentation of key analyses—including information on how adjustments to facility requirements were made—and without correct calculations, stakeholders and decision makers lack reasonable assurances that the replacement medical center will be appropriately sized to meet the needs of the expected beneficiary population in Europe.

DOD's process for developing the approximately $1.2 billion cost estimate for the replacement medical center was substantially consistent with many cost estimating best practices, such as cross-checking major cost elements to confirm similar results. However, DOD minimally documented the data sources, calculations, and estimating methodologies it used in developing the cost estimate. Additionally, DOD anticipates that the new facility will become the hub of a larger medical-services-related campus, for which neither cost estimates nor time frames have yet been developed. Without a cost estimate for the facility that includes detailed documentation, DOD cannot fully demonstrate that the proposed replacement medical center will provide adequate health care capacity at the current estimated cost. Further, DOD and Congress may not have the information they need to make fully informed decisions about the facility.

Contents

Figures

Abbreviations

DOD	Department of Defense
EUCOM	European Command
ICU	intensive-care unit
LEED	Leadership in Energy and Environmental Design
LRMC	Landstuhl Regional Medical Center
MDG	Medical Group
MHS	Military Health System
OMB	Office of Management and Budget
USAG	U.S. Army Garrison

United States Government Accountability Office
Washington, DC 20548

May 25, 2012

The Honorable Tim Johnson
Chairman
The Honorable Mark Kirk
Ranking Member
Subcommittee on Military Construction, Veterans Affairs,
    and Related Agencies
Committee on Appropriations
United States Senate

The Army's Landstuhl Regional Medical Center (LRMC), in Germany, is the Department of Defense's (DOD) only tertiary care medical center in the European Command (EUCOM) area of responsibility. As a tertiary care center, LRMC provides specialized diagnostic and treatment services, such as cardiology and neurosurgery, which are not available at all medical facilities that provide acute inpatient care, for approximately 248,000 beneficiaries, including servicemembers and their families as well as retirees and their families. Wounded servicemembers requiring critical care are medically evacuated from overseas operations—including Afghanistan—to Ramstein Air Base where the 86th Medical Group (MDG) provides them immediate stabilization care on the flight line and then transports them directly to LRMC for definitive care.

Both of these facilities were initially constructed in the 1950s and according to DOD are deficient in meeting the department's life safety and force protection requirements, are out of compliance with many building codes, have limited room in which to expand or renovate, and are undersized to meet current and projected patient workload requirements. In 2008, DOD approved plans to renovate and reconstruct the two facilities at their existing locations. In 2009, the Senate Appropriations Committee directed the department to complete a site assessment and conduct a cost-benefit analysis on the proposed location for the replacement medical center.[1] The Office of the Deputy Under Secretary

---

[1]S. Rep. No. 111-40, at 20-21 (2009). The committee noted that Ramstein Air Base, adjacent to Landstuhl, is the transport hub for combat casualties and could potentially accommodate the new medical center, and directed DOD to conduct a cost-benefit analysis of locating the replacement medical center at its current location or on Ramstein Air Base.

of Defense (Installations and Environment) conducted an analysis, which determined that consolidating the two facilities at one location, at a total estimated cost of $1.2 billion, would be more efficient and cost-effective than renovating both at their current locations. In January 2012, DOD completed the initial design phase of the replacement medical center. However, in December 2011, the Consolidated Appropriations Act, 2012, required that among other things, the Secretary of Defense recertify to the Appropriations Committees in writing that the replacement medical center was properly sized and scoped to meet current and projected health care requirements.[2] During the course of our review, DOD was in the process of conducting this recertification.

DOD is also in the process of reassessing its force structure plans for Europe and is planning to reduce the number of brigade combat teams and the size of the military service component commands in Europe, among other things. Adjustments to DOD posture, in combination with the construction of a new medical center, have raised questions about the appropriate size for the replacement facility as well as the types of services it is to provide. Your subcommittee asked GAO to review DOD's plans for the replacement medical center, including how DOD determined the appropriate size for the facility and the types of services it will need to provide. In response, this report (1) describes how DOD officials considered potential changes to DOD's posture in Europe—and their possible effect on the beneficiary population—when developing facility requirements for the replacement medical center, (2) assesses DOD's process for determining facility requirements for the replacement medical center to determine to what extent it incorporated recently developed quality standards into the facility's design and adhered to DOD guidance, and (3) reviews the process used to develop the cost estimate for the facility to determine to what extent DOD followed established best practices for developing its cost estimate.

To describe how DOD officials considered potential changes to DOD's posture in Europe—and their possible effect on the beneficiary population—when developing facility requirements for the replacement medical center, we obtained available posture planning documentation, including population estimates, and compared it with the beneficiary population data used in planning assumptions for the replacement

---

[2]Pub. L. No. 112-74, 125 Stat. 1138 (2011).

medical center. We met with officials from the Offices of the Assistant Secretary of Defense (Health Affairs) and the Deputy Under Secretary of Defense (Installations and Environment), EUCOM, U.S. Army Europe, and U.S. Air Forces Europe to gain insight into possible scenarios that are being considered for posture changes in Europe. We also discussed with these officials the steps they had taken to ensure the reasonable accuracy of DOD beneficiary data and determined that the data specifically related to the proposed replacement medical center were sufficiently reliable for the purposes of this report.

To assess DOD's process for determining facility requirements for the replacement medical center to determine to what extent it incorporated quality standards into its design and adhered to DOD guidance, we obtained and reviewed documentation used to develop plans for the proposed replacement medical center, such as health care requirements analyses and facility designs. We also reviewed relevant documentation—including checklists—to determine whether DOD included quality and environmentally friendly standards. We also identified key assumptions used to determine facility requirements for the replacement medical center and obtained and reviewed applicable legal and departmental guidance, including DOD instructions and directives, and compared them with the documented assumptions and methods used to develop the facility's requirements. We also met with medical and construction planners at the Office of the Assistant Secretary of Defense (Health Affairs), the TRICARE Management Activity, U.S. Army Medical Command, LRMC, the Air Force Medical Support Agency, and the 86th MDG to discuss how they determined the size of the replacement medical center.

To review the process used to develop the cost estimate for the facility to determine to what extent DOD followed established best practices for developing its cost estimate, we obtained and reviewed available cost estimates for the proposed replacement medical center, as well as supporting documentation. We evaluated this information using GAO's standardized methodology of cost estimating best practices.[3] We determined whether technical baseline documentation exists and is reflected in the estimate. We also discussed project costs with officials

---

[3]GAO, *GAO Cost Estimating and Assessment Guide: Best Practices for Developing and Managing Capital Program Costs*, GAO-09-3SP (Washington, D.C.: March 2009).

from the Office of the Assistant Secretary of Defense (Health Affairs), the TRICARE Management Activity, and the U.S. Army Corps of Engineers, among others.

We conducted this performance audit from July 2011 through May 2012 in accordance with generally accepted government auditing standards. Those standards require that we plan and perform the audit to obtain sufficient, appropriate evidence to provide a reasonable basis for our findings and conclusions based on our audit objectives. We believe that the evidence obtained provides a reasonable basis for our findings and conclusions based on our audit objectives. Further details on our scope and methodology can be found in appendix I.

Background

The Military Health System operated by DOD is large and complex and has a dual health care mission—readiness and benefits. The readiness mission provides medical services and support to the armed forces during contingency operations and involves deploying medical personnel and equipment, as needed, around the world to support military forces. The benefits mission provides medical services and support to members of the armed forces, their family members, and others eligible for DOD health care, such as retired servicemembers and their families.[4] DOD's health care mission is carried out directly through military medical centers, hospitals, and clinics throughout the United States and overseas, commonly referred to as military treatment facilities, as well as by civilian health care providers through TRICARE. Military treatment facilities make up DOD's direct care system for providing health care to beneficiaries.

DOD's delivery of health care services includes, among other things, inpatient and outpatient care. Inpatient care refers to care for a patient who is formally admitted to a hospital or an institution for treatment, or care. Outpatient care, also known as ambulatory care, refers to health

---

[4]Eligible beneficiaries include active duty personnel and their dependents, medically eligible Reserve and National Guard personnel and their dependents, and retirees and their dependents and survivors. TRICARE is the health care program serving active duty servicemembers, National Guard and Reserve members, retirees, their families, survivors, and certain former spouses worldwide. As a major component of the Military Health System, TRICARE brings together the health care resources of the uniformed services and supplements them with networks of civilian health care professionals, institutions, pharmacies, and suppliers to provide access to health care services while also maintaining the capability to support military operations.

care services for an actual or potential disease, injury, or lifestyle-related problem that does not require admission to a medical treatment facility for inpatient care.

The Assistant Secretary of Defense (Health Affairs) is responsible for ensuring the effective execution of DOD's health care mission and exercises authority, direction, and control over medical personnel authorizations and policy, facilities, funding, and other resources within DOD.[5] The TRICARE Management Activity operates under the authority, direction, and control of Health Affairs.

In 2008, the TRICARE Management Activity approved plans to renovate LRMC and the 86th MDG clinic at their existing locations. The initial LRMC plans included renovation of the inpatient tower; construction of an additional tower for emergency medicine, inpatient nursing units, and other clinical and support activities; and demolition of older facilities. The initial plans for the 86th MDG clinic included construction of a single building to consolidate health care services provided at separate facilities that currently make up the 86th MDG clinic. In 2009, the Office of the Deputy Under Secretary of Defense (Installations and Environment), together with Health Affairs, conducted a cost-benefit analysis that included consideration of alternative sites as well as consolidation of the two projects into a single medical center, and determined that consolidating the aging LRMC and 86th MDG clinic into one new facility that provides tertiary care in an area adjacent to Ramstein Air Base, known as the Weilerbach Storage Area, would be more efficient and cost-effective than pursuing two separate renovation or reconstruction projects. The replacement medical center will be operated and maintained by the Army, with the Air Force to provide clinical services that are currently offered at the 86th MDG clinic.

Facility Requirements Process

The version of DOD's guidance governing the planning and acquisition of military health facilities (DOD Instruction 6015.17) that was in effect when the facility requirements for the replacement medical center were determined in 2010 described the procedures to be used by the military

---

[5]For purposes of this report, the Office of the Assistant Secretary of Defense (Health Affairs) will be referred to as Health Affairs.

departments to prepare project proposals for military treatment facilities.[6] This instruction also identified the types of documentation needed to support a project proposal. The documentation includes, among other things, the current and projected beneficiary population served in a military treatment facility's catchment area, as well as current and projected staffing and workload data.[7] Army Medical Command, with input from the Air Force Medical Support Agency, developed a report that summarizes the projected health care requirements for Military Health System beneficiaries in the areas served by the proposed medical center.[8] Generally, the combination of workload data and staffing requirements are key considerations for determining the size and configuration of military treatment facilities. These facility space requirements are identified in a Program for Design document, which lists square footage requirements per medical department and room. The estimated square footage is then used as the basis for developing overall project cost estimates as reflected on DD Form 1391 (Military Construction Project Data), the standard format used throughout DOD to support the planning and execution of military construction projects. Figure 1 provides an illustration of the process used in determining project costs for the replacement medical center.

---

[6]DOD Instruction 6015.17, Planning and Acquisition of Military Health Facilities (Mar. 17, 1983) (canceled by DOD Instruction 6015.17, Military Health System (MHS) Facility Portfolio Management (Jan. 13, 2012)).

[7]Catchment areas are geographic areas determined by the Assistant Secretary of Defense for Health Affairs that are usually within an approximately 40-mile radius of military treatment facilities with inpatient care.

[8]U.S. Army Medical Command, Updated (FY10) Health Care Requirements Analysis (Washington, D.C.: December 2010). The health care requirements analysis report serves as the basis for the planning and programming of the replacement medical center.

Figure 1: Overview of DOD Medical Treatment Facilities Requirements and Project Costs Process

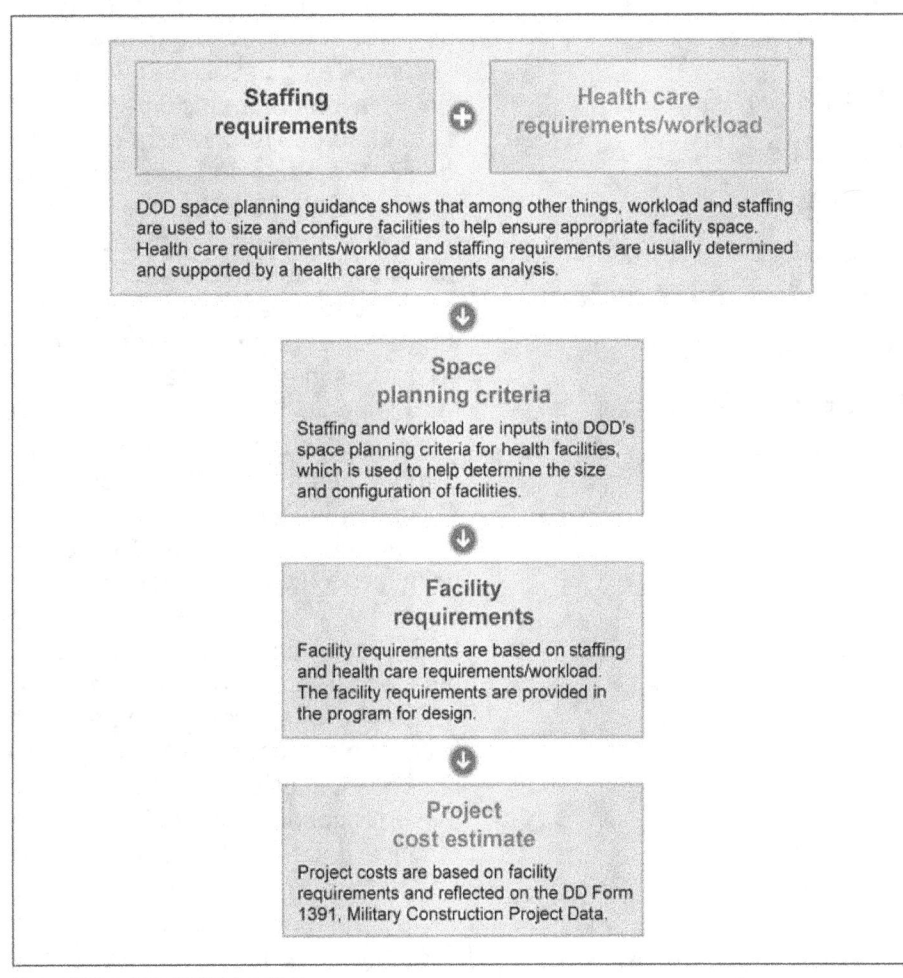

Source: GAO analysis of DOD information.

DOD Considered Beneficiary Data, Contingency Operations, and Posture Changes in Sizing Its Replacement Medical Center but Has Not Assessed More Recent Posture Changes

In planning for the proposed replacement medical center, DOD officials considered beneficiary population data, contingency operations, and changes or expected changes in troop strength known at the time. However, more recent posture changes, announced in January 2012, are currently being assessed by military medical officials for their impact on the replacement medical center. DOD used beneficiary population data as of March 2010 and data on historical patterns of patient migration to identify the areas served by the proposed replacement medical center. A majority of the beneficiaries expected to receive health care from the replacement medical center are located within a 55-mile radius of it. DOD officials told us that because the replacement medical center was designed for peacetime operations—with the capacity to expand to meet the needs of contingency operations—reductions in ongoing contingency operations in Afghanistan would not have an impact on facility requirements.[9] DOD posture in Europe has been reduced over the past few years, and DOD had previously announced that one of four brigade combat teams currently stationed in Europe would be removed by 2015. According to DOD officials, this posture change was not expected to have a significant impact on the size of the replacement medical center because DOD plans to continue to use the facilities at Baumholder, Germany, which will be vacated by the brigade combat team, for other DOD personnel. In January 2012, DOD announced its decision to remove a second brigade combat team currently stationed in Europe, thereby reducing the remaining number of brigade combat teams in Europe to two—one stationed in Germany and the other in Italy. At the time of our review, DOD officials told us that they were in the process of assessing these proposed changes in posture to better understand their ramifications for DOD's medical facility needs.

Beneficiary Population Areas Are Defined Using Historical Patterns of Patient Migration

The replacement medical center will serve as the only tertiary-level referral hospital for the EUCOM, Central Command, and Africa Command theaters of operation. Because of these unique aspects, according to medical planners they did not use typical DOD catchment area standards. Military treatment facilities are typically designed to offer sufficient health care for active duty beneficiaries and their dependents within a 40-mile radius of the military treatment facility. In the case of LRMC, medical

---

[9]The United States ended combat operations in Iraq in August 2010 and completed the removal of most of its troops in December 2011.

planners determined that the historical patterns of care indicated that this area should be a 55-mile radius. Medical planners in the Office of the Secretary of Defense, the Army, and the Air Force analyzed historical patterns of patient migration and contingency operations at LRMC and the 86th MDG to define four catchment areas.[10] See figure 2 for the location of these four catchment areas.

[10]Medical planners are from the TRICARE Management Activity, Portfolio Planning and Management Division; the Army Medical Command, Assistant Chief of Staff for Facilities, Programming and Planning Division; and the Air Force Health Facilities Division.

Figure 2: Location of Four Catchment Areas Used to Define Patient Migration to Landstuhl Regional Medical Center

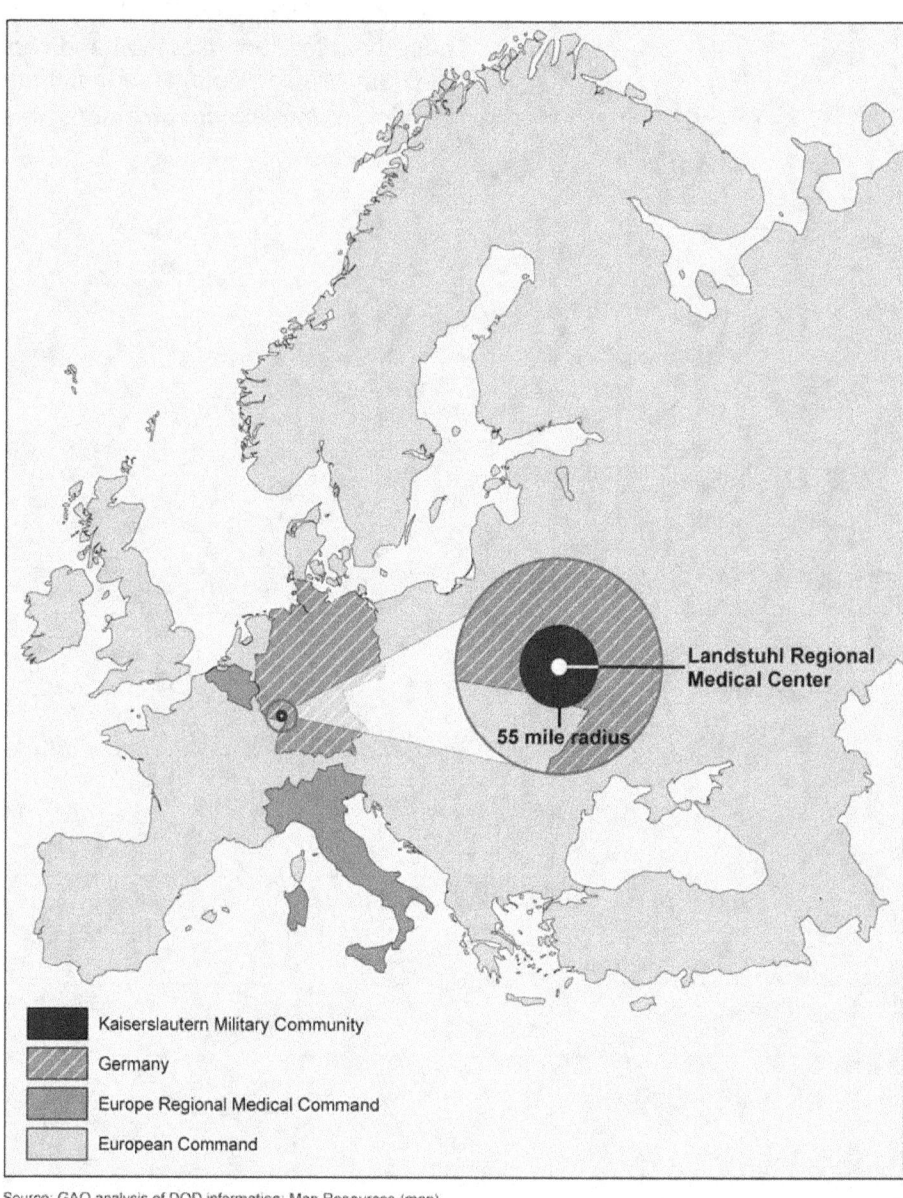

Source: GAO analysis of DOD information; Map Resources (map).

Note: European Command also includes all of Russia, Greenland, and Iceland.

The four catchment areas, as defined by military medical planners, are based on populations of patients who are enrolled as beneficiaries or who are eligible to enroll for the following locations:

1. The Kaiserslautern Military Community catchment area includes all beneficiaries enrolled in LRMC, 86th MDG, and Kleber/Kaiserslautern military treatment facilities. This catchment area is approximately 55-miles in radius surrounding the proposed facility's site.
2. The Germany-wide catchment area includes all beneficiaries enrolled in the Kaiserslautern Military Community catchment area plus beneficiaries enrolled in the military treatment facilities in Germany. This catchment area definition was essential in determining the patterns of enrolled beneficiaries' use of German health care.[11]
3. The Europe Regional Medical Command catchment area includes all beneficiaries in the Germany-wide catchment area plus beneficiaries enrolled in all military treatment facilities in Italy and Belgium. This catchment area reflects historical inpatient referral patterns at LRMC.
4. The EUCOM catchment area includes all enrolled beneficiaries and eligible beneficiaries in Europe, including all beneficiaries in the other three catchment areas.

Table 1 shows the beneficiary population, by catchment area and beneficiary category, as of March 2010. In appendix II we include catchment area populations by beneficiary category, for fiscal years 2006 through 2011.

---

[11]Military beneficiaries are frequently sent to the German health care system because there is not sufficient capacity at LRMC to treat all requirements. This is especially true when there are surges from contingency operations.

Table 1: Landstuhl Regional Medical Center (LRMC) Catchment Areas, by Beneficiary Category, as of March 2010

Catchment area	Beneficiary population			
	Active duty	Active duty family members	Retirees and others[a]	March 2010 total[b]
Kaiserslautern Military Community (enrolled)[c]	13,713	16,781	3,955	**34,449**
Germany-wide (enrolled)	54,460	59,649	11,366	**125,475**
Europe Regional Medical Command (enrolled)[d]	66,068	73,993	13,033	**153,094**
European Command[e] (eligible)[f]	107,818	96,746	43,603	**248,167**

Source: DOD.

[a]"Others" includes retiree family members.

[b]Totals as of March 2010.

[c]An enrolled beneficiary is defined as a TRICARE beneficiary who has elected to receive DOD's managed care options (TRICARE Prime, TRICARE Prime Remote, and TRICARE Prime Remote for Active Duty Family Members, the US Family Health Plan, TRICARE Prime Overseas, or TRICARE Global Remote Overseas) by enrolling in a military treatment facility.

[d]Europe Regional Medical Command consists of beneficiaries enrolled in military treatment facilities located in Germany, Italy, and Belgium. According to DOD analysis, this catchment area reflects historical inpatient referral patterns at LRMC.

[e]The European Command catchment area consists of beneficiaries in TRICARE's Region 13: "Europe." This region includes beneficiaries in both European Command and Central Command.

[f]Eligible beneficiaries include active duty personnel and their dependents, medically eligible Reserve and National Guard personnel and their dependents, and retirees and their dependents and survivors.

According to DOD officials, the flow of patients from theaters of operation, including contingency operations, minimally affects the volume of inpatient care at LRMC and outpatient care at both LRMC and 86th MDG. Table 2 shows that approximately half of all inpatient care at LRMC, a little more than 77 percent of outpatient care at LRMC, and almost 96 percent of outpatient care at the 86th MDG is provided to beneficiaries located within the Kaiserslautern Military Community catchment area as well as the Germany-wide catchment area.

Table 2: Patient Migration Patterns for the Landstuhl Regional Medical Center (LRMC) and the 86th Medical Group (MDG) at Ramstein Air Base in Fiscal Year 2009

Percentages

	Germany-wide catchment area[a]	Europe Regional Medical Command and European Command catchment areas[b]	Contingency operations	Total
LRMC inpatient days of care	49.9	39.6	10.5	**100**
LRMC outpatient encounters	77.3	14.0	8.7	**100**
86th MDG outpatient encounters	95.7	2.7	1.6	**100**

Source: DOD.

[a]The Germany-wide catchment area includes those beneficiaries in the Kaiserslautern Military Community catchment area.

[b]Percentage of inpatient days of care and outpatient encounters for the European Command and Europe Regional Medical Command catchment areas do not include those days of care and encounters from the Germany-wide catchment area.

Replacement Medical Center Is Designed for Peacetime Operations, with Flexible Capacity to Accommodate Contingency Operations

According to DOD officials, the replacement medical center is being sized for peacetime operations, not for contingency operations. However, these officials told us that the replacement medical center is being designed with the flexibility to expand capacity during surges to be able to handle casualties that result from contingency operations.[12]

DOD officials determined that the replacement medical center should be able to accommodate contingency operations' medical needs similar to those experienced in Fallujah, Iraq, during November 2004, in which the United States sustained about 100 casualties and 600 wounded over a 2-month period. For this reason, the new medical center is designed to be able to nearly double its medical/surgical bed capacity if needed to support contingency operations.

According to Army officials, to mitigate the increase in patient workload resulting from surges caused by contingency operations, the new medical center will follow the procedures currently in use at LRMC. These procedures require that priority be given to active duty servicemembers, and therefore, other beneficiaries normally treated at LRMC would be directed to German health care facilities during a time when surge

---

[12]The replacement medical center is designed with 60 single-patient medical/surgical inpatient rooms, 50 of which have the flexibility to expand to accept two beds for surge capacity. We provide a more comprehensive discussion of the medical center's sizing requirements in a later section.

GAO-12-622 Replacement Medical Center at Landstuhl

capability is needed (and capacity is constrained) and then redirected back to LRMC when the workload from contingency operations lessens.

Earlier Posture Reduction Decisions Not Expected to Affect Replacement Medical Center Size, but More Recent Posture Changes Have Yet to Be Evaluated

DOD has been reducing its military posture in Europe since German reunification in 1990. At its peak, the United States had approximately 350,000 active duty servicemembers stationed in EUCOM's area of responsibility. The size of DOD's military posture in EUCOM's area of responsibility is currently estimated at about 78,000 active duty servicemembers. DOD has been reducing its medical treatment capacity over time to correspond to the reduction in the number of military servicemembers stationed in Europe. Today, LRMC is DOD's only remaining tertiary care medical center in Europe. Furthermore, it is the only medical center in Europe, Asia, or Africa that serves beneficiaries from the EUCOM, Central Command, Africa Command, and Special Operations Command areas of responsibility.

In 2004, DOD announced its plans for an overseas basing strategy that called for reducing the number of Army brigade combat teams stationed in Europe from four to two. However, in the February 2010 Quadrennial Defense Review, DOD decided that it would retain all four Army brigade combat teams in Europe, rather than returning two to the United States as originally planned. Moreover, in April 2011, based on several factors, including consultations with allies and the findings of the North Atlantic Treaty Organization's new Strategic Concept, DOD announced that it planned to remove by 2015 only a single brigade combat team from Europe. According to DOD officials, the brigade they anticipated removing from Europe was stationed at U.S. Army Garrison (USAG) Baumholder, Germany, initially leaving brigades at USAG Grafenwoehr and USAG Vilseck, which are located close to one another in Germany and at USAG Vicenza, Italy. There are also elements of the Grafenwoehr brigade at USAG Schweinfurt, Germany. DOD also has plans to eventually close four Army locations in Germany—Heidelberg, Mannheim, Bamberg, and Schweinfurt. As a result of these closures, the elements of the Grafenwoehr brigade at Schweinfurt were expected to move to Grafenwoehr when Schweinfurt closed. As of the date of this report, the four brigade combat teams are still assigned at their original locations in EUCOM. The April 2011 announcement also included a DOD decision to station four Aegis Cruisers in Spain, a change that would increase the military beneficiary population in Europe. Figure 3 shows the locations of DOD military installations in Europe where posture changes are expected to take place that could affect the facility requirements for the replacement medical center.

Figure 3: DOD Military Installations in Europe with Expected Posture Changes That May Affect Replacement Medical Center Facility Requirements

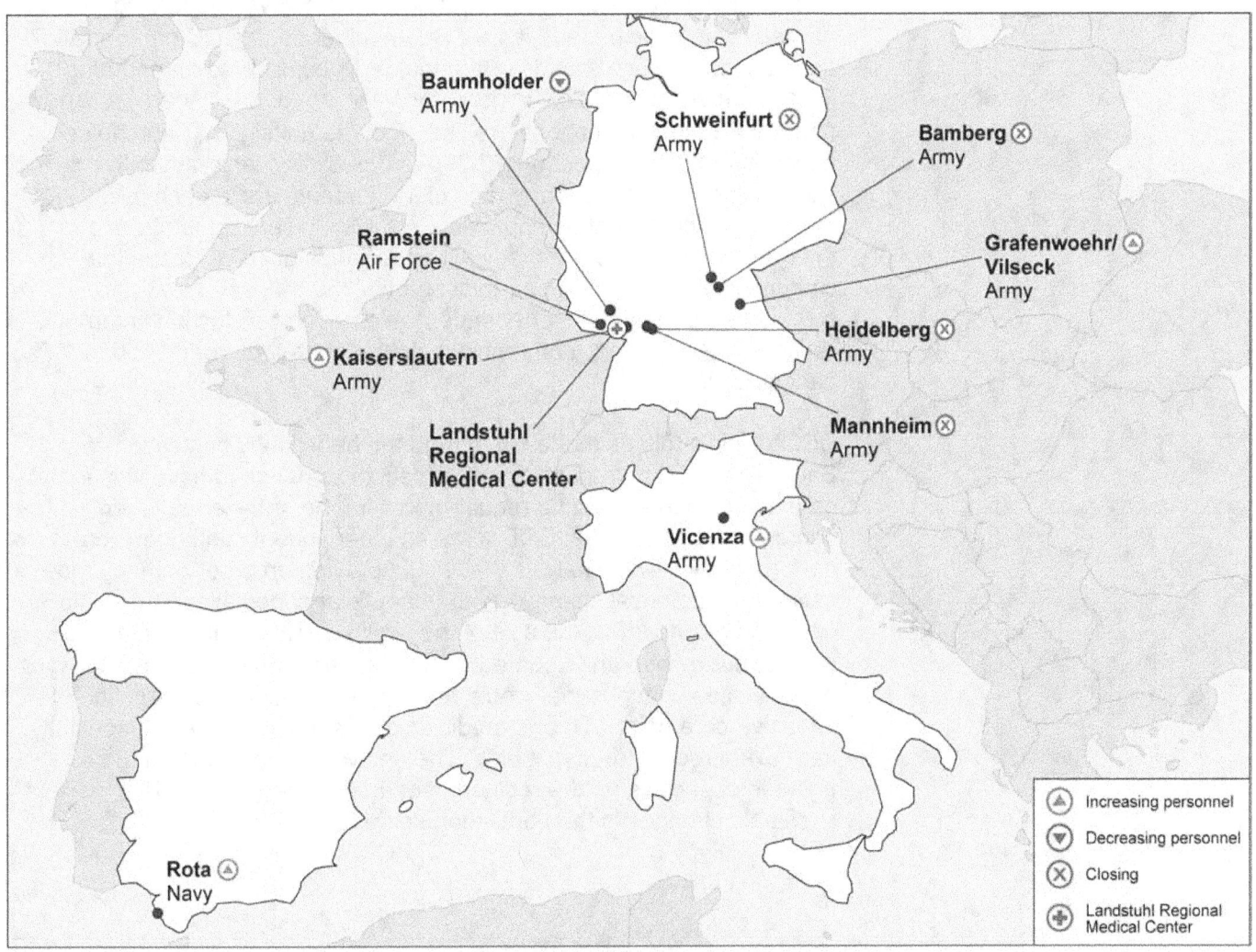

Source: GAO analysis of DOD information; Map Resources (map).

The brigade combat team currently located at Baumholder is within the Kaiserslautern Military Community catchment area and is expected to

GAO-12-622 Replacement Medical Center at Landstuhl

reduce the beneficiary population when it leaves.[13] According to Army officials, the brigade consists of approximately 4,200 soldiers, who are accompanied by about 6,300 dependents.[14] However, according to DOD officials, when this brigade leaves Baumholder other DOD personnel will be restationed there because Baumholder is considered an enduring installation with accessible joint military training facilities nearby.[15] Army officials also told us that because some of the housing at Baumholder is substandard, they expect only 2,300 to 3,500 servicemembers to move to Baumholder. Using the Army ratio of 1.5 dependents to each military member indicates that as approximately 10,500 servicemembers and their dependents who are medical beneficiaries of LRMC leave the catchment area, they will be replaced by 5,750 to 8,750 new servicemembers and their dependents—an overall reduction in the Kaiserslautern Military Community catchment area of from 4,750 to 1,750 beneficiaries.

DOD officials told us that even though the beneficiary population at Baumholder will be reduced, they expect this change to have little impact on the workload and sizing requirements for the replacement medical center. In October 2009, DOD hired an independent contractor, Noblis, to perform a sensitivity analysis that would provide an order of magnitude estimate of potential changes to the beneficiary population that would need to occur to affect the size of the facility.[16] This sensitivity analysis was further refined and updated in 2010. It specifically assessed the type of population changes that would require the addition or subtraction of intensive-care unit (ICU) and medical/surgical beds, as well as specialty care exam rooms for outpatients. The analysis concluded that the planned capacities for the replacement medical center would be resilient to sizable changes in the population served.

---

[13]USAG Baumholder is approximately 17 miles north and west of LRMC, and falls within the Kaiserslautern Military Community catchment area that extends about 55 miles from the facility.

[14]Army officials noted that the Army uses a ratio of 1.5 dependents to each military member to estimate the number of dependents that will be leaving the area.

[15]An enduring installation is one that is permanent and lasting.

[16]Noblis, *Landstuhl Regional Medical Center (LRMC) Sensitivity Analysis* (Oct.29, 2009; updated Aug. 12, 2010).

- A population change of up to 70,000 beneficiaries—a change in the total EUCOM beneficiary population of about 29 percent—would necessitate resizing of the requirements for ICU or medical/surgical beds by the addition or subtraction of a 20-bed module.[17]
- A population change of 25,000 to 31,000 beneficiaries—a change in the total EUCOM beneficiary population of between 10 percent and 13 percent would necessitate re-sizing requirements for specialty care exam rooms by the addition or subtraction of an 8 to 10 exam room module.[18]

DOD officials told us that changes in the beneficiary population are expected to occur in the EUCOM catchment area through 2015. Although some of these changes will increase the population in certain locations, the overall change will be a reduction in the overall number of beneficiaries in EUCOM's area of responsibility. The following beneficiary changes are expected:

- The Army expects a reduction in the Europe Regional Medical Command's active duty servicemembers and their dependents' population of about 21,000—a reduction in the total EUCOM beneficiary population by about 8 percent—by fiscal year 2015, according to the *Updated (FY10) Health Care Requirements Analysis*.[19] However, it does not expect a significant change to the beneficiary population in the immediate Kaiserslautern Military Community catchment area.
- The Air Force does not expect a change in its beneficiary population through fiscal year 2015.
- The Navy expects to gain about 1,200 sailors from the stationing of the Aegis Cruisers in Rota, Spain, along with about 1,300 additional dependents—for a total increase of about 2,500 beneficiaries, or a 1 percent gain in the total EUCOM beneficiary population.

---

[17]According to the Noblis analysis, ICU and medical/surgical beds are typically designed in 20 to 30 bed increments.

[18]According to the Noblis sensitivity analysis, modern health care design calls for modules of 8 to 10 exam rooms.

[19]U.S. Army Medical Command, *Updated (FY10) Health Care Requirements Analysis*. The health care requirements analysis report states that the EUCOM beneficiary population will be reduced by about 10,300 active duty servicemembers and about 10,600 family members.

Based on the results of DOD's 2009 sensitivity analysis, the expected changes would not necessitate a change in the number of ICU beds, medical/surgical beds, or outpatient exam rooms.

In January 2012, however, DOD announced new posture decisions that will further reduce EUCOM's troop strength. According to DOD, these posture decisions are part of a deficit reduction package based on the Budget Control Act of 2011[20] requirement to reduce the department's future expenditures by approximately $487 billion[21] over the next decade. EUCOM data indicate that by 2015 approximately 71,500 active duty military servicemembers will remain in Europe following the latest changes to DOD's European posture.

According to the January 2012 DOD publication *Defense Budget Priorities and Choices*, DOD has updated its April 2011 plans for its European basing strategy and has stated that it intends to now remove two brigade combat teams from Europe.[22] These two brigades are currently located at Baumholder and Grafenwoehr with elements of the brigade in Grafenwoehr located in Schweinfurt. As a result, the elements in Schweinfurt will not relocate to Grafenwoehr as previously planned.

DOD's decision to remove two brigades from Europe and how this shift in troop numbers will affect health care requirements in the EUCOM area of responsibility have yet to be fully determined. However, DOD officials noted that they did not believe the removal of a second brigade combat team would affect the beneficiary population of the replacement medical center because the second brigade is currently stationed outside the immediate Kaiserslautern Military Community catchment area. DOD officials told us that they have started a review to confirm that the shift in DOD posture will not affect the requirements for the proposed replacement medical center. They noted that recent troop reductions are being studied to determine what impact, if any, they will have on the proposed size of the replacement medical center. They also noted that they are developing a sensitivity analysis to accommodate the information and will include it as part of DOD's statutorily required recertification of

---

[20]Pub. L. No. 112-25 (2011).

[21]This number reflects DOD's reported approximation of the reductions required by the Budget Control Act of 2011.

[22]DOD, *Defense Budget Priorities and Choices* (Washington, D.C.: January 2012).

the facility. As of the date of this report, they had not completed the study because along with the recertification, DOD must also submit a plan for implementing GAO's recommendations with respect to the LRMC facility.

DOD Incorporated Quality Standards When Determining Facility Requirements, but Inadequate Documentation Makes It Unclear Whether DOD Adhered to Its Own Guidance

When developing facility requirements for the replacement medical center, DOD officials incorporated many patient quality of care and environmentally friendly design standards. However, our review of the documentation DOD provided in support of these facility requirements revealed gaps, inconsistencies, and calculation errors that required extensive explanation by DOD officials to understand the deviations and decisions made to develop the requirements. Without clear documentation that explains how the analyses were performed and any adjustments made, stakeholders and decision makers lack reasonable assurance that the proposed replacement medical center will be appropriately sized to meet the needs of the expected beneficiary population in Europe.

DOD Incorporated Quality of Care and Environmentally Friendly Design Standards in Determining Facility Requirements

DOD officials used checklists and discussions with external health care providers to incorporate updated patient quality of care standards into the facility requirements for the replacement medical center; they also incorporated environmentally friendly design standards. They used DOD's military hospital construction checklists to ensure that they incorporated updated patient quality of care standards, such as evidence-based design[23] and world-class standards,[24] when determining the size of the replacement medical center. For example, DOD officials told us they used the *Evidence Based Design Checklist*—which DOD created in August 2007 and updated in 2009—to incorporate design concepts into health care construction projects that have impacts on patient-centered care. Examples of evidence-based design include single-patient instead of multiple-patient rooms to better accommodate family involvement in the provision of care and to better control infections, and studying layouts and workspace ergonomics to maximize work pattern efficiency. Additionally, DOD officials and the architectural and engineering firm contracted for the design of the replacement medical center used DOD's *Military Health Service World-Class Checklist* to ensure that world-class standards were integrated into the facility's design. The checklist identifies areas for DOD officials to research to help ensure that world-class standards are systematically developed, validated, and communicated with project teams. The completed checklist described examples of how world-class standards—which encompass many of the evidence-based designs from the *Evidence Based Design Checklist*—were integrated into the facility's design. Some of the world-class standards incorporated into the facility requirements were (1) optimizing the size and position of the patient windows to provide exterior views for the patient from the bed, (2) providing patient and family control over the environment in the patient

---

[23]Evidence-based design represents an emerging body of science that links elements of a facility's design with patient, staff, and resource outcomes. The goal of evidence-based design is to create a healing environment—one that is safe and comfortable and that supports the patient, the patient's family, and the staff. See Noblis, *Evidence-Based Design: Application in the MHS* (Washington, D.C.: Aug. 1, 2007).

[24]In May 2009, the National Capital Region Base Realignment and Closure Health Systems Advisory Subcommittee of the Defense Health Board defined characteristics of a "world-class medical facility" in their report *Achieving World Class*. For example, a world-class facility, among other things, applies evidence-based health care principles and practices, along with the latest advances in the biomedical, informatics, and engineering sciences and organizes its clinical services so that they are integrated and seamless between and among services in the facility. These principles and practices are known as world-class standards.

room (e.g., heating and cooling), and (3) providing full height walls with higher noise transmission ratings (a higher noise transmission rating blocks more noise from transmitting through a wall) in spaces where patients would be asked to disclose personal information. DOD officials told us they also met with officials from Department of Veterans Affairs' hospitals, private sector hospitals, and German hospitals to obtain information on evidence-based practices for providing health care that could be applied to the replacement medical center's design.

DOD has also incorporated additional environmental and efficiency features into the design of the replacement medical center and expects to exceed the U.S. Green Building Council's Leadership in Energy and Environmental Design (LEED) green building standards, which have been adopted by several federal agencies.[25] The LEED system awards points for meeting a variety of standards and certifies buildings as silver, gold, or platinum. The replacement medical center's current design will likely qualify for a "silver" certification. However, the facility's extensive energy efficiency and renewable energy features indicate that it may qualify for a "gold" certification once it has met the more stringent German design requirements. For example, the project will use low water plumbing fixtures and commercial kitchen equipment available in Germany to reduce water use and achieve higher efficiency.

Inconsistencies, Gaps, and Calculation Errors in Planning Documentation Make It Unclear Whether DOD Adhered to Its Own Guidance for Determining Facility Requirements

DOD sized the replacement medical center based on projected patient workload data. However, our review of the planning documentation DOD provided in support of its facility requirements showed that there were (1) inconsistencies in how DOD projected patient workload and applied the planning criteria, (2) some areas where the planning documentation did not clearly show how DOD officials had applied the formulas provided in the criteria to generate requirements, and (3) calculation errors throughout. DOD guidance in effect when the facility was designed[26] provided that when designing medical facilities, planners should develop

---

[25]LEED is a third-party certification program and the nationally accepted benchmark for the design, construction, and operation of high-performance green buildings, according to the nonprofit U.S. Green Building Council.

[26]DOD Instruction 6015.17, *Planning and Acquisition of Military Health Facilities* (Mar. 17, 1983) (cancelled by DOD Instruction 6015.17, *Military Health System (MHS) Facility Portfolio Management* (Jan. 13, 2012)).

patient workload factors[27]—both current and projected—and use these factors to determine the sizing requirements for the facility. While DOD officials acknowledged that inconsistencies, gaps in documentation, and calculation errors existed in the requirements documentation, they did not think the identified issues alone would necessitate a revision of the facility requirements. However, because DOD has not yet determined the effects of the newly proposed posture changes on projected patient workload—which in turn drives the requirement for the facility size—it is not known if the inconsistencies, gaps, and calculation errors coupled with the posture change will require DOD to revise its facility requirements. DOD officials plan to examine these concerns in their recertification process.

The *Updated (FY10) Health Care Requirements Analysis* report for LRMC captures some of these data and steps DOD used to determine the sizing requirements for the replacement medical center (see table 3 for the sizing requirements that DOD developed, by medical center department).[28]

---

[27]Workload factors include the workload for inpatient and outpatient care. For example, the average daily census can be used to measure workload for inpatient care, and the number of outpatient encounters can be used to measure workload for outpatient care.

[28]The *Updated (FY10) Health Care Requirements Analysis* describes the analyses conducted to determine the requirements for the replacement medical center.

Table 3: Proposed Sizing Requirements for the Replacement Medical Center

Department	Number of beds	Number of rooms
Inpatient beds		
Intensive care unit	18	
Newborn intensive care unit	8	
Medical/surgical	60[a]	
Obstetrician-postpartum	14	
Behavioral health	30	
Total number of inpatient beds	**130**	
Operating rooms		9
Labor and delivery rooms		6
Outpatient exam rooms		198

Sources: GAO (analysis); DOD (data).

[a]Fifty of the 60 single-patient medical/surgical inpatient beds have the capability to become semiprivate patient rooms if needed for surge capacity, which would bring the total number of beds to 180 if all 50 were placed in service.

Inconsistencies in projecting workload and applying criteria. To project most inpatient and outpatient workload for the replacement medical center, DOD officials used fiscal year 2010 estimated patient workload data as a baseline.[29] However, they used different baseline data in different parts of the analysis. For example, in determining the number of labor and delivery rooms, DOD officials did not use workload data from fiscal year 2010 as the baseline. According to DOD officials, the obstetrician workload has historically been relatively stable. Therefore, they used the labor and delivery room workload data from the *Health Care Requirements Analysis*, which had been conducted in fiscal year 2008 to support the original plan for renovating and reconstructing LRMC and determined that the data were accurate enough for their purposes.

Once DOD officials determined what projected workload data to use in their calculations for the new facility, they were to use the criteria in *DOD Space Planning Criteria for Health Facilities* to calculate the facility's requirements, for example, the appropriate number of inpatient beds and

---

[29]DOD developed the fiscal year 2010 baseline for both the inpatient and outpatient care workload by annualizing the actual workload from the first 6 months of fiscal year 2010— the most recent available at the time.

GAO-12-622 Replacement Medical Center at Landstuhl

outpatient exam rooms.[30] DOD officials generally used the formulas provided in this document, but they applied them inconsistently when determining the appropriate size for individual departments within the facility. For example, the space planning criteria direct DOD officials to divide an inpatient department's projected workload—in this case, the average daily census—by a particular occupancy rate to determine the number of inpatient beds that would be required.[31] The criteria specify that certain inpatient beds should be designed in modules of 4, 6, or 8 beds. DOD generally followed these criteria in calculating the number of nursing unit medical/surgical beds, a type of inpatient bed. The criteria specify an occupancy rate of 85 percent for inpatient medical/surgical beds. Following this formula, DOD officials divided the projected average daily census (48.7 patients) by 0.85. This calculation resulted in a requirement for 57.3 beds. To conform to the modular grouping criteria, DOD officials rounded to 60 beds.

However, in determining the number of inpatient behavioral health beds DOD officials deviated from these criteria. The projected average daily census for behavioral health was 24 patients. The space planning criteria specify a 70 percent occupancy rate for psychiatric (i.e., behavioral health) beds when the average daily census is fewer than 25 patients, instead of the 85 percent occupancy rate specified for nursing unit medical/surgical beds. Nevertheless, DOD officials used an 85 percent occupancy rate to calculate the requirement for behavioral health beds. This resulted in a requirement for 28.2 beds—rounded to 30 beds to conform to the modular grouping criteria. According to DOD officials, they chose to use a different occupancy rate factor because they reasoned that since space planning criteria had not been updated to reflect the shift to single occupancy rooms, the 70 percent rate would likely result in a requirement for a higher number of beds. Following the space planning criteria's guidance would have produced a requirement for 34.3 beds,

---

[30]The guidance shows that among other things, workload and staffing are used to size and configure facilities to help ensure appropriate facility space. Specifically, the guidance provides formulas for determining the appropriate size of patient care departments, such as the required number of medical/surgical beds or behavioral health beds, using the projected workload data for the facility.

[31]The average daily census identifies the "average" number of patients occupying beds at a specific hospital site as determined by the inpatient census at midnight but does not specify the actual number of beds to be planned to ensure that a bed is available on any given day. This requires the application of a planned occupancy rate. Occupancy rates are stated as a percentage (e.g., 80 percent or 0.80).

which would have been rounded to 36 beds to account for the modular grouping criteria. As a result, the need for behavioral health beds may actually be higher than DOD officials determined. The documentation did not clearly convey the reasons for the deviations or adjustments DOD officials made when applying the criteria, and as a result, decision makers may lack reasonable assurances that the number of beds required would be sufficient to meet the needs of the expected beneficiary population in Europe. Although these deviations or adjustments may not adversely affect the size of the replacement medical center, their effect when combined with the yet to be assessed posture changes remains unknown.

Inadequate documentation of how facility requirements were estimated. DOD's documentation of its processes for determining the replacement medical center's sizing requirements did not always clearly indicate how DOD officials had generated these requirements and omitted details that would have helped demonstrate how DOD officials had determined the size of the replacement medical center. For example, DOD's planning documentation reported contradictory methods for projecting patient workload. According to the *Updated (FY10) Health Care Requirements Analysis*, DOD used three different scenarios to project the facility's workload, resulting in a low, a midrange, and a high projection; all three scenarios used estimated patient workload data from fiscal year 2010 as the baseline:

- Scenario A excluded the workload attributable to the conflicts in Iraq and Afghanistan, and assumed that the change in patient workload would continue to follow the trend set over the previous 5 years.[32]
- Scenario B adjusted for potential future decreases in beneficiary population, and assumed that the change in patient workload would continue to follow the trend set over the previous 5 years.[33]
- Scenario C assumed that the change in patient workload would continue to follow the trend set over the previous 5 years and made no exclusions or adjustments.

---

[32]The health care requirements analysis report notes that approximately 10.5 percent of inpatient care and 8.7 percent of outpatient care provided at the current facilities was based on conflicts in Iraq and Afghanistan.

[33]In July 2010, the Army projected a decrease of approximately 21,000 beneficiaries, or 8 percent of the population.

The *Updated (FY10) Health Care Requirements Analysis* first reported using Scenario B—the scenario that resulted in midrange projections—to project inpatient and outpatient workload for the replacement facility. However, later sections of the document report the use of different methods to project patient workload. DOD officials confirmed that they had used a combination of methods to project inpatient and outpatient workload, and that they had used Scenario B only to validate these projections after they had calculated them. These officials acknowledged that the *Updated (FY10) Health Care Requirements Analysis* could have better documented how these projections were developed. The lack of clear documentation makes it difficult to understand the processes used without extensive explanation by DOD officials.

In addition, the *Updated (FY10) Health Care Requirements Analysis* omitted details on how DOD officials developed certain data. For example, the document does not show how DOD officials projected inpatient workload for behavioral health beds, only noting that the projected average daily census was 24 patients. Although the *Updated (FY10) Health Care Requirements Analysis* did not document how the average daily census was calculated, DOD officials told us that the historical data on inpatient behavioral health workload were not sufficient for projecting workload because LRMC's behavioral health inpatient capacity was such that any beneficiaries other than active duty servicemembers were referred to the German economy for treatment. Therefore, the officials said they used another method (Scenario C) to project workload, so that the facility would have the inpatient behavioral health capacity to treat additional patients. The planning documentation also does not show how DOD officials projected the number of providers required for outpatient ambulatory departments.[34] The *Updated (FY10) Health Care Requirements Analysis* contains a table with the number of outpatient ambulatory providers but does not show how or whether projected outpatient workload data for the replacement medical center were used to determine the number of outpatient providers that would be required. These gaps in documentation make it unclear whether the size of the replacement medical center will be adequate to meet the needs of the beneficiary population, and when combined with potential posture

---

[34]Unlike inpatient bed requirements, which are based on projected patient workload data, outpatient exam room requirements are based on the number of providers needed to treat the projected outpatient workload.

changes and previously discussed deviations or adjustments, the extent to which they may affect the size of the facility is unknown.

Calculation errors in the planning documentation. We also found several calculation errors within the *Updated (FY10) Health Care Requirements Analysis* report. One table in the report that shows historical (5-year average), baseline, and projected workload for inpatient and outpatient care had errors in the 5-year average column for inpatient dispositions[35] and bed days of care. When we spoke with DOD officials, we pointed out these errors. DOD officials acknowledged the errors and noted that the correct numbers could be found in a separate table in the report's appendix—although the appendix table was not listed as a reference to support the historical workload numbers. Additionally, a table in the report's appendix, which illustrated the different projected inpatient and outpatient workload data, calculated using the three different scenarios, had many calculation errors in the projected outpatient workload columns. Specifically, in calculating projected workload using Scenarios A and B, DOD incorrectly used the 5-year average—instead of the fiscal year 2010 data—as a baseline, and when using Scenario C, DOD adjusted for potential decreases in the beneficiary population, although this scenario did not call for such an adjustment. As a result, outpatient workload data using Scenario B, for example, was calculated to be 288,534 encounters instead of 328,944 (a 14 percent difference). The projected data derived by incorrectly applying Scenario B were then used in another table in the report's appendix to verify that the projected outpatient provider staffing would be sufficient to treat the projected number of outpatients. DOD officials acknowledged the error and provided us with correct data. According to DOD officials, even though there was a 14 percent difference in the projected outpatient workload data, the outpatient provider staffing levels would still be sufficient. Although these calculation errors may not adversely affect the size of the replacement medical center, it remains unknown to what extent this error will affect facility requirements when combined with the yet to be assessed posture changes, previously discussed deviations or adjustments, and gaps in documentation.

---

[35]The number of inpatient dispositions, also known as inpatient encounters, is a measurement of inpatient workload.

Standards for internal controls include, among other things, control activities.[36] Control activities include policies, procedures, techniques, and mechanisms that enforce management's directives. They can include a wide range of activities—such as authorizations, verifications, and documentation—that should be readily available for examination. Detailed and appropriate documentation is a key component of internal controls. Without clear documentation of key analyses, and of how adjustments to facility requirements were made, stakeholders lack reasonable assurances that the proposed replacement medical center will be able to provide the appropriate health care capacity to meet the needs of the beneficiary population it is expected to serve.

DOD's Cost Estimate Was Not Well Documented and Cost Elements for Associated Facilities Have Yet to Be Developed

In developing the cost estimate for the replacement facility, DOD followed many of the best practices in developing estimates of capital projects, but DOD minimally documented the data sources, calculations, and estimating methodologies used in developing the cost estimate. Further, it is anticipated that the replacement medical center will become the hub of a larger medical-services-related campus, for which neither cost estimates nor time frames have yet been developed.

DOD's Cost Estimation Methodology Substantially Met Best Practice Criteria but Was Not Well Documented

The *GAO Cost Estimating and Assessment Guide* contains cost estimating best practices that have been identified by GAO and cost experts within organizations throughout the federal government and industry.[37] These best practices can be grouped into four general characteristics of sound cost estimating:

1. "Accurate" refers to being unbiased and ensuring that the cost estimating is not overly conservative or overly optimistic and is based on an assessment of most likely costs.

---

[36]GAO, *Standards for Internal Control in the Federal Government*, GAO/AIMD-00-21.3.1 (Washington, D.C.: November 1999).

[37]GAO-09-3SP. The guide establishes a consistent methodology that is based on best practices and can be used across the federal government for developing, managing, and evaluating capital program cost estimates.

2. "Credible" refers to discussing any limitations of the analysis because of uncertainty or bias surrounding data or assumptions used in the cost estimating process.
3. "Comprehensive" refers to ensuring that cost elements are neither omitted nor double counted, and all cost-influencing ground rules and assumptions are detailed.
4. "Well documented" refers to thoroughly documenting the process, including source data and significance, clearly detailed calculations and results, and explanations of why particular methods and references were chosen.

See appendix III for detailed information on each of these cost estimating characteristics.

In addition, Office of Management and Budget (OMB) best practices note that programs should maintain current and well-documented estimates of program costs, and that these estimates should encompass the full life cycle of the program.[38]

The characteristics of sound cost estimating are divided into individual criteria, which we used to assess DOD's process for developing its cost estimate. Our process for evaluating the cost estimate consisted of assigning an assessment rating for the various criteria evaluated on a 1 to 5 scale: not met = 1, minimally met = 2, partially met = 3, substantially met = 4, and met = 5. Then, we took the average of the individual assessment ratings to determine an overall rating for each of the overarching characteristics: accurate, credible, comprehensive, and well documented. Criteria assessed as not applicable were not given a score and were not included in our calculation of the overall assessment. Furthermore, our review of DOD's process for developing the cost estimate does not reflect an assessment of how facility requirements were developed or their quality, but only a determination of whether they are described in technical documentation and reflected in the estimate.[39] However, as discussed previously in this report, during our assessment of

---

[38]OMB, *Capital Programming Guide: Supplement to Circular A-11, Part 7, Preparation, Submission, and Execution of the Budget* (Washington, D.C.: June 2006).

[39]Technical documentation refers to documents used to define technical and programmatic requirements for the replacement medical center, such as beneficiary population estimates, health care demand, staffing requirements, and square footage requirements.

DOD's process for determining facility requirements for the replacement medical center, we found some calculation errors in the facility requirements.

Table 4 provides a summary of our assessment of DOD's cost estimating process.

Table 4: Summary Assessment of the Results of DOD Cost Estimating Process for the Replacement Medical Center as Compared to Best Practices

Characteristic	Overall assessment[a]	Best practice	Individual assessment
Accurate	Substantially met	The cost estimate results are unbiased, not overly conservative or optimistic, and based on an assessment of the most likely costs.	Minimally met
		The estimate has been adjusted properly for inflation.	Partially met
		The estimate contains few, if any, minor mistakes.	Met
		The cost estimate is regularly updated to reflect significant changes in the program so that it always reflects current status.	Met
		Variances between planned and actual costs are documented, explained, and reviewed.	Not applicable
		The estimate is based on a historical record of cost estimating and actual experiences from other comparable programs.	Substantially met
Credible	Substantially met	The cost estimate includes a sensitivity analysis that identifies a range of possible costs based on varying major assumptions, parameters, and data inputs.	Partially met
		A risk and uncertainty analysis has been conducted that quantified the imperfectly understood risks and identified the effects of changing key cost driver assumptions and factors.	Partially met
		Major cost elements have been cross-checked to see whether results were similar.	Met
		An independent cost estimate has been conducted by a group outside the acquiring organization to determine whether other estimating methods produce similar results.	Met
Comprehensive	Substantially met	The cost estimate includes all life cycle costs.	Minimally met
		The cost estimate completely defines the program, reflects the current schedule, and is technically reasonable.	Substantially met
		The cost estimate work breakdown structure is product oriented, traceable to the statement of work/objective, and at an appropriate level of detail to ensure that cost elements are neither omitted nor double counted.[b]	Met
		The estimate documents all cost-influencing ground rules and assumptions.	
Well documented	Minimally met	The documentation captures the source data used, the reliability of the data, and how the data were normalized.	Minimally met

Characteristic	Overall assessment[a]	Best practice	Individual assessment
		The documentation describes in sufficient detail the calculations performed and the estimating methodology used to derive each element's cost.	Minimally met
		The documentation describes step-by-step how the estimate was developed, so that a cost analyst unfamiliar with the program would be able to understand what had been done and replicate it.	Minimally met
		The documentation discusses the technical baseline description and the data in the baseline are consistent with the estimate.	Minimally met
		The documentation provides evidence that the cost estimate has been reviewed and accepted by management.	Partially met

Source: GAO analysis of DOD data.

[a]Assessments are defined as follows: not met means that DOD provided no evidence that satisfies the criterion; minimally met means that DOD provided evidence that satisfies a small portion of the criterion, but overall, did not include sufficient support for stakeholders to reasonably conclude that the cost estimate is reliable; partially met means that DOD provided evidence that satisfies about half of the criterion; substantially met means that DOD provided evidence that satisfies a large portion of the criterion; and met means that DOD provided complete evidence that satisfies the entire criterion.

[b]A work breakdown defines in detail the work necessary to accomplish a program's objectives. It deconstructs a program's end product into successive levels with smaller specific elements until the work is subdivided to a level suitable for management control. It is also a valuable communication tool between management and stakeholders because it provides a clear picture of what needs to be accomplished and how the work will be done. In addition, it provides a consistent framework for planning and assigning responsibility for the work. Initially set up when the program is established, the work breakdown structure becomes more detailed over time, as more information becomes known about the program.

DOD's Cost Estimating Methodology for the Replacement Medical Center Substantially Met Best Practice Criteria for Accuracy

We determined that the cost estimate for the replacement medical center had been updated as project requirements were better defined. The overall cost estimate was broken down into costs per square foot, which were based on historical records of costs and actual experiences from other comparable programs. Although the DD Form 1391 does not include documentation regarding how inflation was factored into the estimated costs for the replacement medical center, DOD officials told us that costs on the DD Form 1391 have been adjusted for inflation using departmental guidance.

We found no evidence indicating that the cost estimate is biased. However, it is not possible to fully assess the accuracy and reliability of a cost estimate without conducting a risk analysis that indicates the confidence level associated with the project's estimated cost. Yet, the independent estimate and estimate validation that are further described below are sufficient to meet the requirements of this criterion.

DOD's Cost Estimating Methodology for the Replacement Medical Center Substantially Met Best Practice Criteria for Credibility Overall, but Lacked Sensitivity and Risk Analyses of Some Key Cost Elements

DOD hired an architecture and engineering firm to validate the cost estimate using a cross-check of major cost elements to determine whether alternative methods would have produced similar results.[40] The contractor concluded that the cost estimate was valid. It also developed an independent cost estimate and determined that the design of the facility was within 1 percent of the size listed on the DD Form 1391, and that the resulting cost was also within 1 percent of DOD's cost estimate.[41]

DOD officials told us that they also hired a separate firm to develop sensitivity and risk analyses that were designed to meet GAO cost estimating standards as published in the *Cost Estimating and Assessment Guide*.[42] However, we found some limitations in these analyses. The only cost drivers evaluated were the exchange rate, German inflation, the cost of various raw materials, and a composite labor rate. The analyses did not evaluate the potential cost impact of variations in the beneficiary population, catchment area, level of care provided, or amount of battle-related injuries. Moreover, the analyses did not evaluate the cost impact of varying the square footage requirements documented in the Program for Design.[43] To determine whether an estimate is credible, key cost elements should be tested for sensitivity, and other cost estimating techniques should be used to cross-check the reasonableness of the ground rules and assumptions. It is also important to determine how sensitive the final results are to changes in key assumptions and parameters.

---

[40]HOK, *Kaiserslautern Military Community Medical Center Charrette Report* (March 2011).

[41]HOK, *Kaiserslautern Military Community Medical Center Charrette Report.*

[42]United States Army Corps of Engineers Europe District and Booz Allen Hamilton, *Sensitivity Analysis and Cost/Schedule Probability Report for Kaiserslautern Military Community Medical Center* (January 2012).

[43]The Program for Design is a document used by DOD when determining facility requirements for military treatment facilities that lists footage requirements per medical department and room.

DOD's Cost Estimating Methodology for the Replacement Medical Center Substantially Met Best Practice Criteria for Comprehensiveness Overall, but Lacked Recurring Life Cycle Costs

DOD's cost estimating methodology for the replacement medical center substantially met best practice criteria for overall comprehensiveness, but some costs and assumptions were not included in the individual criteria that make up the comprehensive cost estimating characteristic. The cost estimate generally includes categories of costs for the design, construction, and outfitting of the replacement medical center. Additionally, DOD provided an appropriate work breakdown structure for the facility to help ensure that cost elements were neither omitted nor double counted.

DOD also provided us with technical baseline documentation, including the *Updated (FY10) Health Care Requirements Analysis* report and the Program for Design, which defines the technical and programmatic requirements of the project. DOD officials told us that technical baseline documentation was developed by qualified personnel—including a multidisciplinary team of health care planners, architects, and engineers—and has been updated as the project has evolved. We found no instances in which any costs for design, construction, and outfitting of the replacement medical center were omitted.

Although DOD provided us with some cost information as well as technical baseline documentation, additional recurring life cycle costs were, for the most part, not available, resulting in this subcategory criterion for comprehensiveness being rated as minimally met. The cost estimate does not include any facility sustainment costs, costs for supporting infrastructure, or any operation and maintenance costs for personnel or equipment required to operate the facility. In addition, the cost estimate does not include costs associated with the disposition or retirement of proposed medical center facilities at the end of their life cycles, such as demolition or renovation costs. In addition, DOD officials said costs associated with the disposition of the current LRMC or 86th MDG are not included in the cost estimate. Army officials told us that the facilities that make up the current LRMC will remain under the auspices of the Army. These officials noted that following completion of the replacement medical center, ownership of the current LRMC facilities will transfer to Army Installation and Management Command. Under this arrangement, these facilities will no longer be classified as part of the Military Health System. Therefore, Army officials told us that any costs associated with their disposition should not be included in the overall estimate for the replacement medical center. The 86th MDG clinic consists of 13 separate buildings. The remaining components that make up the current 86th MDG clinic will be transferred to Ramstein Air Base. According to 86th MDG officials, some of these buildings will remain in use following completion of the replacement medical center, while others will be demolished. However, it has not been decided how the remaining clinic buildings will be used; the officials said that this decision will be made by the installation commander at Ramstein Air Base. Since demolition or continued use of the remaining facilities will require DOD funding, these costs should be captured; they will help to show the full cost impact of the replacement medical center project. Further, the cost estimate contains minimal documentation of cost-influencing ground rules and assumptions. DOD officials noted that some of the ground rules and assumptions have been included in the technical baseline documentation. However, we could not find a documented reference or link in the technical baseline documentation we examined to specific cost elements in the DD Form 1391. We also found no evidence of documentation of the risks associated with assumptions, which should be traced to specific cost elements.

A life cycle cost estimate should encompass all past (or sunk), present, and future costs for every aspect of the program, regardless of funding source, including all government and contractor costs. Without a full accounting of life cycle costs, management will have difficulty successfully planning program resource requirements and making wise decisions about where to allocate resources. Cost estimates are typically based on limited information and therefore need to be bound by the constraints that make estimating possible. These constraints are usually defined by ground rules and assumptions. However, because such assumptions are best guesses, the risks associated with a change to any of these assumptions must be identified and assessed. Many assumptions profoundly influence cost; the subsequent rejection of even a single assumption could invalidate many aspects of the cost estimate. Unless ground rules and assumptions are clearly documented, a cost estimate will not provide a basis for developing resolutions concerning areas of potential risk. Furthermore, it will not be possible to reconstruct the estimate when the original estimators are no longer available.

DOD's Cost Estimating Methodology for the Replacement Medical Center Minimally Met Best Practice Criteria for Well Documented

A well-documented cost estimate is essential if an effective independent review is to ensure that it is valid. However, the documentation DOD provided in support of its cost estimate did not clearly demonstrate how facility requirements had been factored into cost elements.

DOD's cost estimate lacked documentation that described, in detail, the calculations performed and the estimating methodology used to derive the cost for each element of the replacement medical center. None of the documents provided to us included detailed documentation of how DOD developed and refined the cost estimate. A complete documentation of source data would include, for each line item in the cost estimate, a reference to a specific data source or sources (including the document and page number) used as the basis for each square footage and unit cost amount. For example, the cost estimate contains line item estimates for electricity, water/sewer/gas, steam/chilled water distribution, and storm drainage. However, from the documentation provided, it is not possible to determine how these requirements were used to develop cost estimates.

The technical baseline description and data in the technical baseline documentation are spread across several documents, including the *Updated (FY10) Health Care Requirements Analysis* report, Program for Design, and a Planning Charrette Discussion.[44] However, only the Planning Charrette Discussion is referenced in the cost estimate on the DD Form 1391. Moreover, we found minor differences between the square footage requirements in the Program for Design and the cost estimate as described on the DD Form 1391. For example, the Program for Design reports a total gross square footage requirement of 1,293,409 and the cost estimate reports a total requirement of 1,340,731 square feet. It was not possible to compare square footage amounts for various components of the facility because of the differing levels of detail in the Program for Design and the cost estimate. The difference in square footage numbers between the Program for Design and the DD Form 1391 is not documented; therefore, the reasons for the difference are unclear. Since the technical baseline is intended to serve as the basis for developing a cost estimate, it should be discussed in the cost estimate documentation.

Cost estimators should provide a briefing to management about how the estimate was constructed—including specific details about the program's technical characteristics, assumptions, data, cost estimating methodologies, sensitivity, risk, and uncertainty—so management can gain confidence that the estimate is accurate, complete, and high in quality. However, we found no documentation of a detailed review and approval that included the estimate's technical foundation, ground rules and assumptions, estimating methods, data sources, sensitivity analysis,

---

[44]The Planning Charrette Discussion is a document that summarizes information from a series of meetings that DOD planners held from May 10 through 12, 2010, to adjust preliminary programming and facility scoping for the replacement medical center in order to address the on-the-ground situation and any previously unforeseen issues.

risks and uncertainty, cost drivers, cost phasing, contingency reserves, or affordability.

DOD officials confirmed our conclusion that their cost estimating process was not fully documented. They told us that they had developed supporting facility costs using expert opinion and parametric models; however, these were not listed in the cost estimate.[45] According to DOD officials, DOD guidance does not require detailed documentation as part of the DD Form 1391 cost estimate. Under DOD's cost methodology, as the project design matures, so does the level of cost analysis. DOD officials asserted that the current cost estimate is appropriate for the current level of design. DOD officials acknowledged that better documentation would have provided more support and information to the various decision makers in the process and would be a good practice to follow.

If the cost estimate for the replacement medical center does not include detailed documentation, stakeholders cannot reasonably conclude that it is reliable. In addition, DOD and Congress may not have the information they need to make fully informed decisions about the facility. If a cost estimate does not fully account for life cycle costs, management will have difficulty successfully planning program resource requirements and making wise decisions. Poorly documented cost estimates can cause a program's credibility to suffer, because the documentation cannot explain the rationale of the methodology or the calculations underlying the cost elements. Further, without clear technical baseline documentation, the cost estimate will not be based on a comprehensive program description and will lack specific information regarding technical and program risks. Unless the cost estimate is fully documented, it cannot be reconciled with an independent cost estimate.

---

[45]Parametric models typically consist of several interrelated cost estimates and are often computerized. They may involve extensive use of cost-to-noncost cost estimating relationships, multiple independent variables related to a single cost effect, or independent variables defined in terms of design characteristics rather than more discrete material requirements or production processes. Parametric models are always useful for cross-checking the reasonableness of a cost estimate that is derived by other means. As a primary estimating method, parametric models are most appropriate during the engineering concept phase when requirements are still somewhat unclear and no bill of materials exists.

Replacement Medical Center Expected to Be Part of Medical Campus, but Additional Cost Elements Have Yet to Be Determined

DOD officials told us that the replacement medical center will be a fully functioning military treatment facility and not require any additional support facilities to fulfill its mission of providing inpatient and outpatient care. However, in the Strategic Concept of Operations section of the *Updated (FY10) Health Care Requirements Analysis* report for the replacement medical center, the center is described as being the hub of a medical-services-related campus at Weilerbach Storage Area.[46] The medical campus is expected to be an integrated health care campus that would include hospital and ancillary components as well as outpatient, administrative, and educational components. The other facilities that DOD expects to develop for this campus under separate military projects include warrior transition unit facilities, medical transition detachment housing, and possibly medical troop barracks, among other facilities.

At this time, DOD has not determined the additional costs for these facilities, nor has it developed a time frame for their construction. However, Army officials told us that plans for the campus concept are still predecisional and that certain facilities would only be replicated at Weilerbach Storage Area following the expiration of their useful life. For instance, the child care center near the current LRMC will remain there until it requires renovation or reconstruction. At that point, a similar facility would be constructed at Weilerbach Storage Area to replace it, so that staff working at the replacement medical center would not have to leave the area for day care services for their children.

Conclusions

The need to replace the outdated LRMC and the 86th MDG clinic to ensure that military servicemembers and their families receive the care they deserve is widely recognized. A critical step toward meeting this goal is the development of a credible and comprehensive assessment of the facility requirements and the cost of the replacement medical center. DOD's evolving posture in Europe will likely have an impact on the size of the beneficiary population served by the replacement medical center. However, DOD's current needs assessment contains inconsistencies and errors in how it used patient workload and staffing data to determine facility requirements, such as facility size. In several situations, DOD officials adjusted the criteria being used but failed to document their rationale or need for taking these steps. Moreover, the documentation

---

[46]U.S. Army Medical Command, *Updated (FY10) Health Care Requirements Analysis.*

used to support the determination of the facility requirements does not clearly describe the methodology or calculations used to develop the requirements, and these requirements provided the basis for the cost estimate. DOD officials have indicated that the issues GAO has identified may not have a substantial impact on the size of the replacement medical center, but they have not yet taken specific action to determine what the individual or cumulative effects would be. DOD's cost estimating methodology substantially met many best practices criteria but was only minimally documented. Congress has required the Secretary of Defense recertify to the Appropriations Committees in writing that the replacement medical center is properly sized and scoped to meet current and projected health care requirements. With this recertification, DOD has an opportunity to determine the impact the proposed posture changes will have on the proposed facility requirements and revise its documentation to provide clear support for how it developed its facility requirements. Without clear documentation of how key requirements were developed and how they factored into the development of facility requirements and cost, DOD cannot fully demonstrate that the proposed replacement medical center will provide adequate health care capacity at the current estimated cost.

Recommendations for Executive Action

To ensure that the replacement medical center is appropriately sized to meet the health care needs of beneficiaries in a cost-effective manner, we recommend that as part of the facility's recertification process, the Secretary of Defense direct the Assistant Secretary of Defense (Health Affairs) to take the following two actions:

- provide sufficient and clear documentation on how medical planners applied DOD criteria to determine the facility's requirements, including how and why medical planners made adjustments to the criteria, and
- correct any calculation errors and show what impact, if any, these errors had on the sizing of the facility.

Furthermore, in light of recently announced posture changes and potential adjustments that may need to be made in facility requirements based on correcting identified calculation errors in the original documentation, we recommend that the Secretary of Defense direct the Assistant Secretary of Defense (Health Affairs) to revise the cost estimate for the center, incorporating the best practices outlined in the GAO Cost Estimating and Assessment Guide to

- reflect these potential posture changes,

- update it with the revised calculations as part of the recertification process, and
- more thoroughly document the data, assumptions, calculations, and methodology used to develop specific cost elements.

Agency Comments and Our Evaluation

In written comments to a draft of this report, DOD agreed with our conclusions and each of our recommendations. DOD stated that it recently conducted a reassessment of the original $1.2 billion project submitted in the Fiscal Year 2012 President's Budget request that responds to GAO's recommendations by utilizing the most current data, including recently announced force structure changes, and providing a documented audit trail of how the size, scope, and cost of the alternatives were developed. Although we are encouraged that DOD has performed a reassessment, DOD did not make it available for our review. DOD's comments noted that the reassessment will be provided once approved by the Secretary of Defense. As a result, we are unable to confirm at this time that these actions have been taken. Therefore, we believe our recommendations are still appropriate until the reassessment is released and documentation made available.

DOD also provided technical and clarifying comments, which we incorporated as appropriate into this report. DOD's comments are reprinted in their entirety in appendix IV.

We are sending copies of this report to the interested congressional committees, Secretary of Defense; the Secretaries of the Army and the Air Force; and the Director of the Office of Management and Budget. In addition, the report is available at no charge on the GAO website at http://www.gao.gov.

If you or your staff have any questions about this report, please contact us at (202) 512-7968 or mctiguej@gao.gov or (202) 512-7114 or draperd@gao.gov. Contact points for our Offices of Congressional Relations and Public Affairs may be found on the last page of this report. GAO staff who made key contributions to this report are listed in appendix V.

James R. McTigue, Jr.
Director, Defense Capabilities and
  Management

Debra A. Draper
Director, Health Care

Appendix I: Objectives, Scope, and Methodology

To describe how DOD officials considered potential changes to DOD's posture in Europe—and their possible effect on the beneficiary population—when developing facility requirements for the replacement medical center, we obtained available posture planning documentation, including population estimates, and compared it with the beneficiary population data used in planning assumptions for the replacement medical center. We also obtained and reviewed Health Care Requirements Analysis documentation containing beneficiary population information and requested and reviewed more recent updates of this information. We met with officials from the Offices of the Assistant Secretary of Defense (Health Affairs) and the Deputy Under Secretary of Defense (Installations and Environment), U.S. European Command, U.S. Army Europe, and U.S. Air Forces Europe to gain insight into possible scenarios that are being considered for posture changes in Europe. In addition we talked with some of the above individuals and met with officials with the U.S. Army Corps of Engineers Europe and with the U.S. Army Installation Command Europe to discuss how the location for the replacement medical center was selected. We also discussed with some of the officials above the steps they had taken to ensure reasonable accuracy of DOD beneficiary data and determined that the data specifically related to the proposed replacement medical center were sufficiently reliable for the purposes of this report.

To assess DOD's process for determining facility requirements for the replacement medical center to determine to what extent it incorporated quality standards into its design and adhered to DOD guidance, we obtained and reviewed documents detailing the process and any data used in the development of the requirements for the replacement facility. Specifically, we obtained and reviewed documentation used to develop plans for the proposed replacement medical center, such as health care requirements analyses and facility designs. We also reviewed relevant documentation—including checklists—to determine whether DOD included quality and environmentally friendly standards, such as world-class standards and Leadership in Energy and Environmental Design (LEED) green building standards.[1] We also identified key assumptions used to determine facility requirements for the replacement medical center and obtained and reviewed applicable legal and departmental

---

[1] LEED is a third-party certification program and the nationally accepted benchmark for the design, construction, and operation of high-performance green buildings, according to the nonprofit U.S. Green Building Council.

guidance, including DOD instructions and directives, and compared them with the documented assumptions and methods used to develop the facility's requirements. Additionally, we reviewed their facility requirements documentation for calculation errors and attempted to duplicate their results. We also met with medical and construction planners with the Office of the Assistant Secretary of Defense (Health Affairs), the TRICARE Management Activity, U.S. Army Medical Command, the Landstuhl Regional Medical Center (LRMC), the Air Force Medical Support Agency, and the 86th Medical Group (MDG) to discuss how they determined the size of the replacement medical center.

To review the process used to develop the cost estimate for the facility to determine to what extent DOD followed established best practices for developing its cost estimate, we obtained and reviewed available cost estimates for the proposed replacement medical center as well as supporting documentation that was used to determine overall costs. We evaluated this information using GAO's standardized methodology of cost estimating best practices. For our reporting needs, we collapsed these best practices into four general characteristics for sound cost estimating: accurate, credible, comprehensive, and well documented. We determined the overall assessment by rating whether DOD followed best practices that make up each of the four characteristics. We assigned a number to our ratings: not met = 1, minimally met = 2, partially met =3, substantially met = 4, and met = 5. We took the average of the individual assessment ratings to determine the overall rating for each of the four characteristics. Criteria assessed as not applicable were not given a score and not included in the overall assessment calculation. We met with officials from the Office of the Assistant Secretary of Defense (Health Affairs), the TRICARE Management Activity, Army Medical Command, the Air Force Medical Support Agency, and the U.S. Army Corps of Engineers prior to our evaluation to explain our approach for reviewing DOD's cost estimating process and to discuss project costs. We also met with these officials to discuss the results of our evaluation. To determine the overall costs of the replacement medical center, we obtained and reviewed planning documents. We also met with officials from LRMC and 86th MDG to discuss what the future plans are for the current facilities following construction of the replacement medical center.

We conducted this performance audit from July 2011 through May 2012 in accordance with generally accepted government auditing standards. Those standards require that we plan and perform the audit to obtain sufficient, appropriate evidence to provide a reasonable basis for our findings and conclusions based on our audit objectives. We believe that

the evidence obtained provides a reasonable basis for our findings and
conclusions based on our audit objectives.

Appendix II: Catchment Area Populations by Beneficiary Category, Fiscal Years 2006 through 2011

Beneficiaries	2006	2007	2008	2009	2010	2011
Kaiserslautern Military Community enrolled						
Active duty	13,614	12,828	13,365	13,970	13,452	13,833
Active duty family member	16,453	15,749	16,218	16,695	16,576	17,338
Retiree	1,551	1,636	1,687	1,603	1,837	1,976
Other	1,922	2,079	2,128	2,038	2,340	2,599
Total	33,540	32,292	33,398	34,306	34,205	35,746
Germany enrolled						
Active duty	65,966	59,247	55,758	56,074	54,633	54,982
Active duty family member	68,299	62,505	60,204	60,081	58,872	59,512
Retiree	5,280	5,439	5,321	4,791	5,038	5,110
Other	6,946	7,229	7,124	6,283	6,488	6,579
Total	146,491	134,420	128,407	127,229	125,031	126,183
Europe Regional Medical Command enrolled						
Active duty	78,390	71,166	67,380	67,578	66,275	66,609
Active duty family member	82,795	76,807	74,522	74,471	72,548	73,030
Retiree	5,807	6,006	5,892	5,411	5,708	5,767
Other	7,743	8,076	7,989	7,238	7,491	7,555
Total	174,735	162,055	155,783	154,698	152,022	152,961
European Command elligible						
Active duty	103,383	95,436	90,713	115,516	110,568	112,031
Active duty family member	108,889	101,188	98,445	97,507	94,911	92,037
Retiree	14,294	14,435	14,343	14,703	14,498	14,447
Other	28,160	27,597	26,827	27,593	28,449	28,444
Total	254,726	238,656	230,328	255,319	248,426	246,959

Source: GAO analysis of DOD information.

Appendix III: Detailed Information on Each of the Cost Estimating Characteristics

The *GAO Cost Estimating and Assessment Guide* contains cost estimating best practices that have been identified by GAO and cost experts within organizations throughout the federal government and industry.[1] For our reporting needs, we collapsed these best practices into four general characteristics of sound cost estimating: accuracy, credibility, comprehensiveness, and well documented. Table 5 provides detailed information on each of these cost estimating characteristics.

Table 5: Characteristics of High-Quality and Reliable Cost Estimates

Characteristic	Description
Accurate	The cost estimate should provide for results that are unbiased, and it should not be overly conservative or optimistic. An estimate is accurate when it is based on an assessment of most likely costs, adjusted properly for inflation, and contains few, if any, minor mistakes. In addition, a cost estimate should be updated regularly to reflect significant changes in the program, such as when schedules or other assumptions change, and actual costs, so that it is always reflecting current status. During the update process, variances between planned and actual costs should be documented, explained, and reviewed. Among other things, the estimate should be grounded in a historical record of cost estimating and actual experiences on other comparable programs.
Credible	The cost estimate should discuss any limitations of the analysis because of uncertainty or biases surrounding data or assumptions. Major assumptions should be varied, and other outcomes recomputed to determine how sensitive they are to changes in the assumptions. Risk and uncertainty analysis should be performed to determine the level of risk associated with the estimate. Further, the estimate's cost drivers should be cross-checked, and an independent cost estimate conducted by a group outside the acquiring organization should be developed to determine whether other estimating methods produce similar results.
Comprehensive	The cost estimate should include both government and contractor costs of the program over its full life cycle, from inception of the program through design, development, deployment, and operation and maintenance to retirement of the program. The cost estimate should also completely define the program, reflect the current schedule, and be technically reasonable. Comprehensive cost estimates should be structured in sufficient detail to ensure that cost elements are neither omitted nor double counted. Specifically, the cost estimate should be based on a product-oriented work breakdown structure that allows a program to track cost and schedule by defined deliverables, such as hardware or software components.[a] Finally, where information is limited and judgments must be made, the cost estimate should document all cost-influencing ground rules and assumptions.

[1]GAO-09-3SP. The guide establishes a consistent methodology that is based on best practices and can be used across the federal government for developing, managing, and evaluating capital program cost estimates.

Characteristic	Description
Well documented	A good cost estimate, while taking the form of a single number, is supported by detailed documentation that describes how it was derived and how the expected funding will be spent in order to achieve a given objective. Therefore, the documentation should capture in writing such things as the source data used, the calculations performed and their results, and the estimating methodology used to derive each work breakdown structure element's cost. Moreover, this information should be captured in such a way that the data used to derive the estimate can be traced back to and verified against their sources so that the estimate can be easily replicated and updated. The documentation should also discuss the program requirements and scope and how the data were normalized. Finally, the documentation should include evidence that the cost estimate was reviewed and accepted by management.

Source: GAO.

[a] A work breakdown defines in detail the work necessary to accomplish a program's objectives. It deconstructs a program's end product into successive levels with smaller specific elements until the work is subdivided to a level suitable for management control. It is also a valuable communication tool between management and stakeholders because it provides a clear picture of what needs to be accomplished and how the work will be done. In addition, it provides a consistent framework for planning and assigning responsibility for the work. Initially set up when the program is established, the work breakdown structure becomes more detailed over time, as more information becomes known about the program.

Appendix IV: Comments from the Department of Defense

THE ASSISTANT SECRETARY OF DEFENSE

1200 DEFENSE PENTAGON
WASHINGTON, DC 20301-1200

HEALTH AFFAIRS

Mr. James R. McTigue, Jr.
Acting Director, Defense Capabilities
   and Management
U.S. Government Accountability Office
441 G Street, N.W.
Washington, DC 20548

Dear Mr. McTigue:

This is the Department of Defense's (DoD) response to the Government Accountability Office (GAO) Draft Report, GAO-12-622, "DEFENSE INFRASTRUCTURE: Documentation Lacking to Fully Support How DoD Determined Specifications for the Landstuhl Replacement Medical Center," dated April 20, 2012, (GAO Code 35163). Thank you for the opportunity to review the Draft Report and offer comments.

Overall, I concur with the Draft Report and its conclusions. However, as you know, the Department recently conducted a reassessment of the original $1.2 billion project submitted in the Fiscal Year 2012 President's Budget request. This new analysis was conducted in a manner separate and independent of the analysis reviewed by GAO. It responds to GAO's recommendations by utilizing the most current data, including recently announced force structure changes, and providing a documented audit trail of how the size, scope, and cost of the alternatives were developed. It does not attempt to adjust or re-interpret previous planning documentation. The final DoD Reassessment Report will be provided once approved by the Secretary of Defense.

Thank you again for the opportunity to review and provide a response. The points of contact on this issue are Mr. John Becker (Functional) and Mr. Gunther Zimmerman (Audit Liaison). Mr. Becker may be reached at (703) 681-4368, and Mr. Zimmerman may be reached at (703) 681-4360.

Thank you for your interest in the health and well-being of our Service members, veterans, and their families.

Sincerely,

Jonathan Woodson, M.D.

.

GAO DRAFT REPORT DATED APRIL 20, 2012
GAO-12-622 (GAO CODE 351630)

"DEFENSE INFRASTRUCTURE: DOCUMENTATION LACKING TO FULLY
SUPPORT HOW DOD DETERMINED SPECIFICATION FOR THE
LANDSTUHL REPLACEMENT MEDICAL CENTER"

DEPARTMENT OF DEFENSE COMMENTS
TO THE GAO RECOMMENDATIONS

RECOMMENDATION 1: The GAO recommends that the Secretary of Defense direct
the Assistant Secretary of Defense (Health Affairs) to provide sufficient and clear
documentation on how medical planners applied DoD criteria to determine the facility's
requirements, including how and why medical planners made adjustments to the criteria.
(See page 42/GAO Draft Report.)

DoD RESPONSE: Concur. DoD acknowledges that there are some deficiencies in the
documentation of the HCRA, including deviations from published criteria. While the
planning team may have had legitimate reasons for making adjustments, assumptions and
data used to draw conclusions about facility sizing are not always clearly documented.
DoD believes that the recently completed re-assessment addresses these issues. The
assumptions that serve as the basis for sizing three courses of action (COA) are clearly
stated. Data trails are explicit and when there are deviations from existing criteria, a
rationale is provided.

RECOMMENDATION 2: The GAO recommends that the Secretary of Defense direct
the Assistant Secretary of Defense (Health Affairs) to correct any calculation errors and
show what impact, if any, these errors had on the sizing of the facility. (See page
42/GAO Draft Report.)

DoD RESPONSE. Concur. DoD acknowledges that the HCRA contained some
calculation errors. However, their characterization as "errors throughout" may not
accurately reflect their actual frequency. All calculations have since been re-computed as
part of the recently completed re-assessment and efforts have been made to ensure their
accuracy and consistency. Accordingly, the likelihood of similar calculation errors in the

re-assessment is extremely low. Sizing of the COAs in the re-assessment are based on a
series of calculations that can be readily duplicated and confirmed.

RECOMMENDATION 3: The GAO recommends that the Secretary of Defense direct
the Assistant Secretary of Defense (Health Affairs) to revise the cost estimate for the
center, incorporating the best practices outlined in the GAO's Cost Estimating and
Assessment Guide to: reflect these potential posture changes; update it with the revised
calculations as part of the recertification process; and more thoroughly document the
data, assumptions, calculations, and methodology used to develop specific cost elements
(See page 42/GAO Draft Report.)

DoD RESPONSE: Concur. The facility acquisition and life cycle costs have been
revised to reflect force structure changes known as of 1 May 2012. Sizing is based on
revised calculations that accurately reflect projected population and workload. The
impact of these changes on space requirements have been addressed and reflected in the
COAs. Data assumptions, calculations, and methodology have been documented in a
manner more consistent with the GAO Cost Estimating and Assessment Guide. It should
be noted that DoD was unaware of this guidance until August of 2011, long after the cost
estimate was developed for the current project submitted in the FY 2012 President's
Budget.

Appendix V: GAO Contacts and Staff Acknowledgments

GAO Contacts	James R. McTigue, Jr., (202) 512-7968 or mctiguej@gao.gov Debra A. Draper, (202) 512-7114 or draperd@gao.gov
Staff Acknowledgments	In addition to the contacts named above, Laura Durland, Assistant Director; Marcia Mann, Assistant Director; Josh Margraf; Jeff Mayhew; and Richard Meeks made key contributions to this report. Joanne Landesman assisted in the message and report development, Amie Steele assisted in developing the report's tables and graphics, Jennifer Echard and Dave Brown provided methodological support, and Michael Willems provided legal support.